Read
Trace
Write
a
une
l
je
am
un m
an
une
as
comme
at
à
AF415742

Read and write the sentence!

a	This is a bird.
I	I will play with the toys.
am	I am crawling on the ground.
an	This is an ant.
as	It is as light as a feather.
at	She is at her friend's house.

Read
Trace
Write
be
être
by
par
do
faire
go
aller
he
il
if
si

Read and write the sentence!

be	We will be friends.
by	This story is by me.
do	She will do the cleaning.
go	He will go somewhere.
he	He is bored.
if	If I put my clothes here, it will get washed.

Read   Trace   Write

Read and write the sentence!

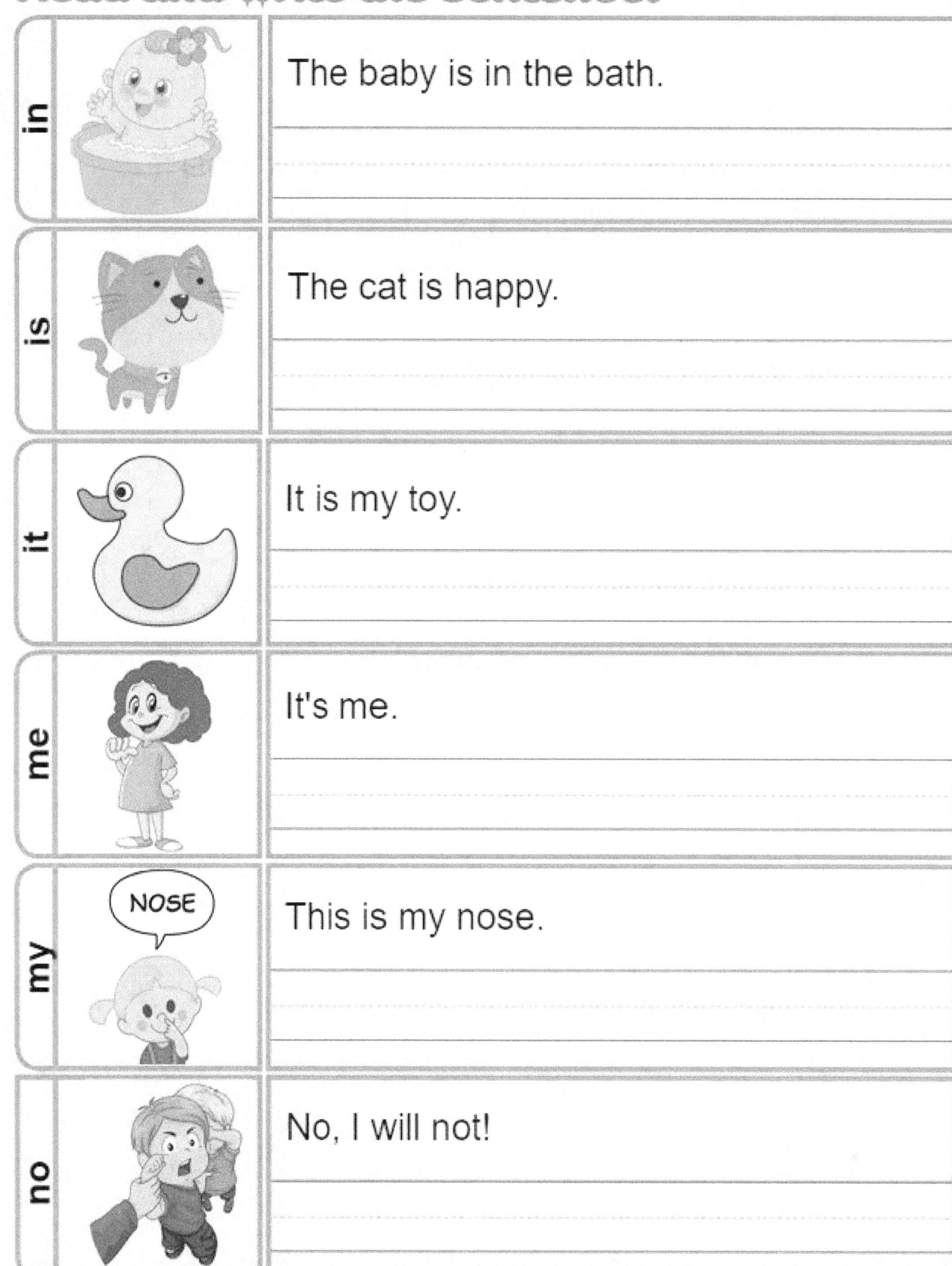

in	The baby is in the bath.
is	The cat is happy.
it	It is my toy.
me	It's me.
my	This is my nose.
no	No, I will not!

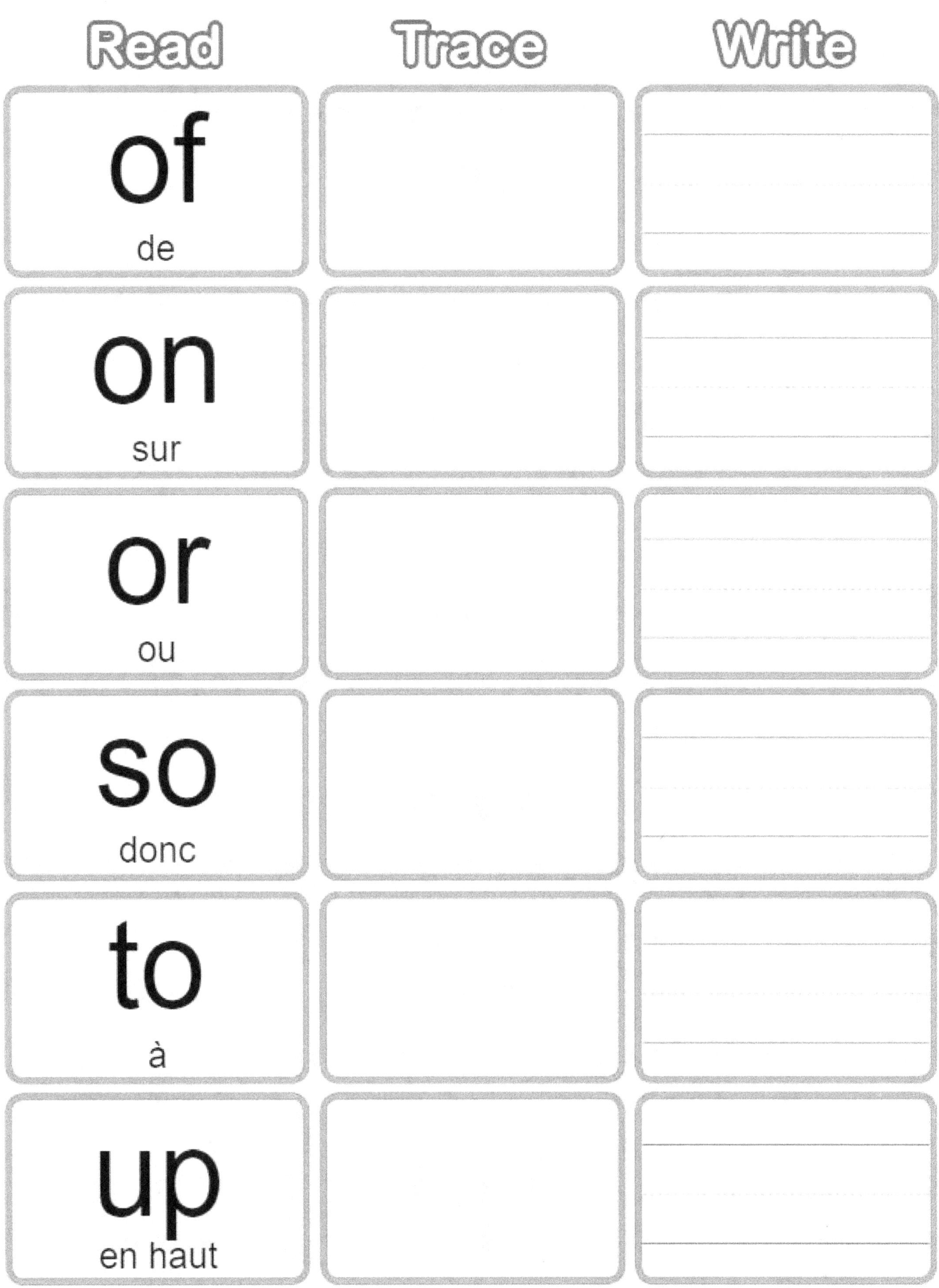

Read
Trace
Write
of
de
on
sur
or
ou
so
donc
to
à
up
en haut

Read and write the sentence!

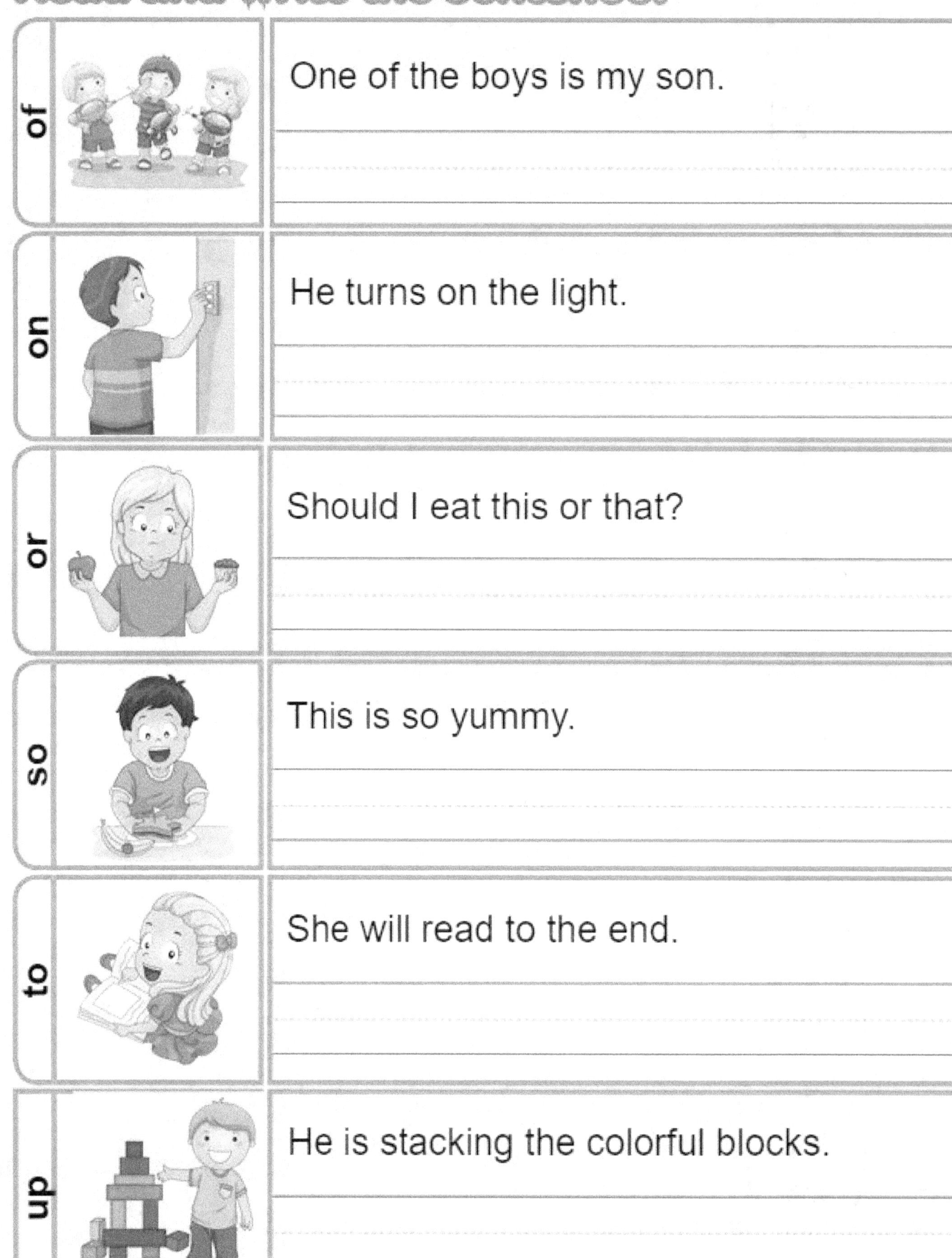

of		One of the boys is my son.
on		He turns on the light.
or		Should I eat this or that?
so		This is so yummy.
to		She will read to the end.
up		He is stacking the colorful blocks.

Read	Trace	Write
us nous		
we nous		
all tout		
and et		
any tout		
are sont		

Read and write the sentence!

us		Both of us are walking.
we		We are helping to make a house.
all		We are all dancing together.
and		My brother and I are playing.
any		They can read any books.
are		The eggs are colorful.

Read
Trace
Write
ask
demander
ate
a mangé
bed
lit
big
gros
box
boîte
boy
garçon

Read and write the sentence!

ask
The girl asks a question.

ate
They ate yummy ice cream.

bed
This bed is for the baby.

big
The bottle is very big.

box
The box has all my toys.

boy
The boy is hiding behind it.

Read	Trace	Write
but mais		
buy acheter		
can pouvez		
car voiture		
cat chat		
cow vache		

Read and write the sentence!

but		I want to go, but my son doesn't.
buy		He buys lots of stuff.
can		The baby will drink milk from the can.
car		The car is red.
cat		The cat is sad.
cow		The cow is funny.

Read
Trace
Write
cut
couper
day
journée
did
fait
dog
chien
eat
manger
egg
oeuf

Read and write the sentence!

Read
Trace
Write
eye
œil
far
loin
fly
mouche
for
pour
get
avoir
got
eu

Read and write the sentence!

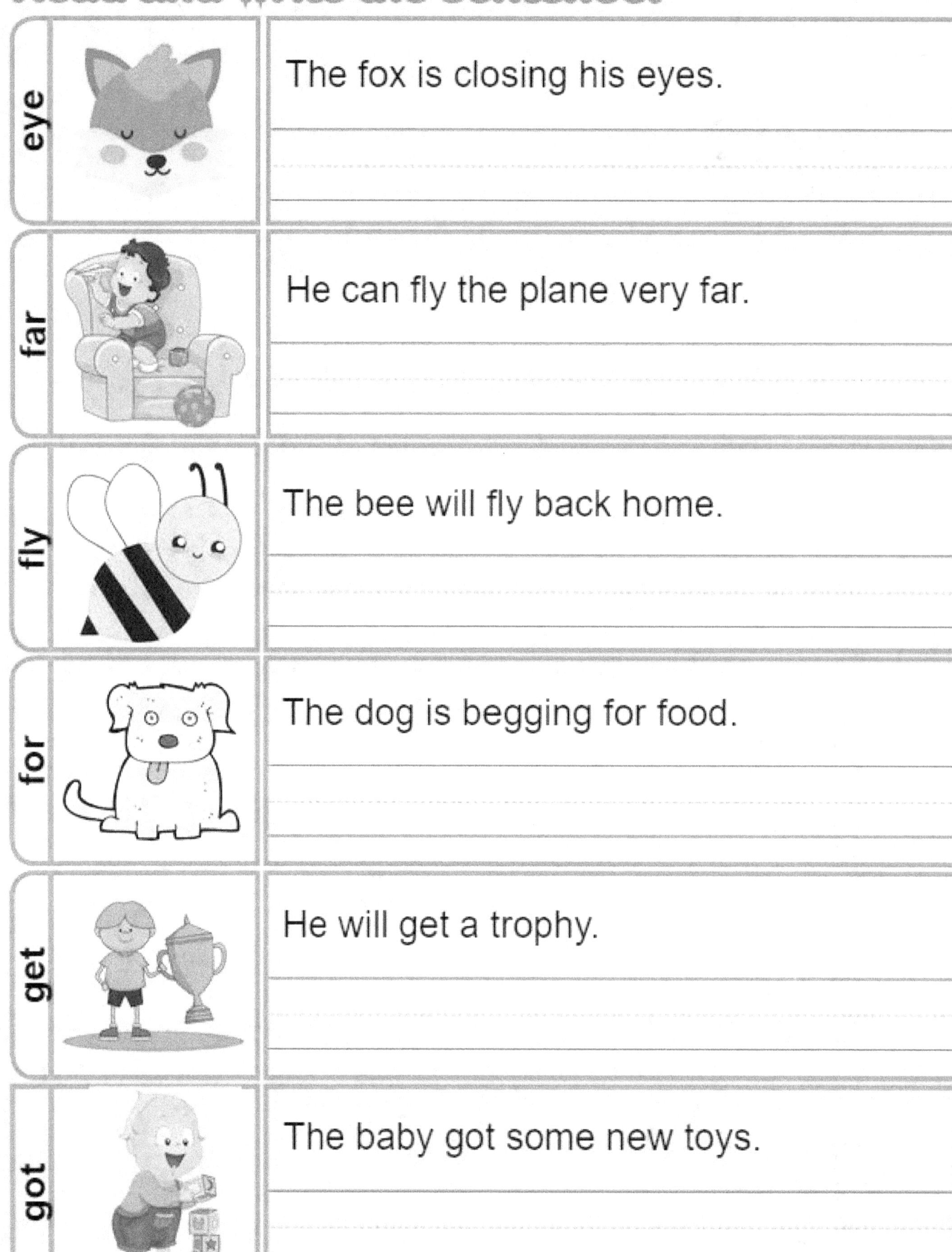

eye		The fox is closing his eyes.
far		He can fly the plane very far.
fly		The bee will fly back home.
for		The dog is begging for food.
get		He will get a trophy.
got		The baby got some new toys.

Read
Trace
Write
had
eu
has
a
her
sa
him
lui
his
le sien
hot
chaud

had		He had a big tummy.
has		She has a doll.
her		She has her trolley.
him		I gave my hat to him.
his		His cheeks are big.
hot		It is hot on the beach.

Read — Trace — Write

Read and write the sentence!

how	How many blocks are there?
its	Its legs are short.
leg	His legs are short.
let	Let me come in!
man	The man is a vet.
may	May I have more?

Read	Trace	Write
men hommes		
new nouveau		
not ne pas		
now maintenant		
off de		
old vieux		

The men are mining for gold.

She has a new hat.

She is not feeling well.

Now I am doing my homework.

They cut off the paper.

You are one year old!

Read	Trace	Write
one une		
our notre		
out en dehors		
own posséder		
pig porc		
put mettre		

Read and write the sentence!

one	The panda says one.
our	This is our room.
out	He will go out.
own	The man owns a computer.
pig	She is sleeping on her pig.
put	She is putting an arm around her daughter.

Read | Trace | Write

Read	Trace	Write
ran courir		
red rouge		
run courir		
saw voir		
say dire		
see voir		

Read and write the sentence!

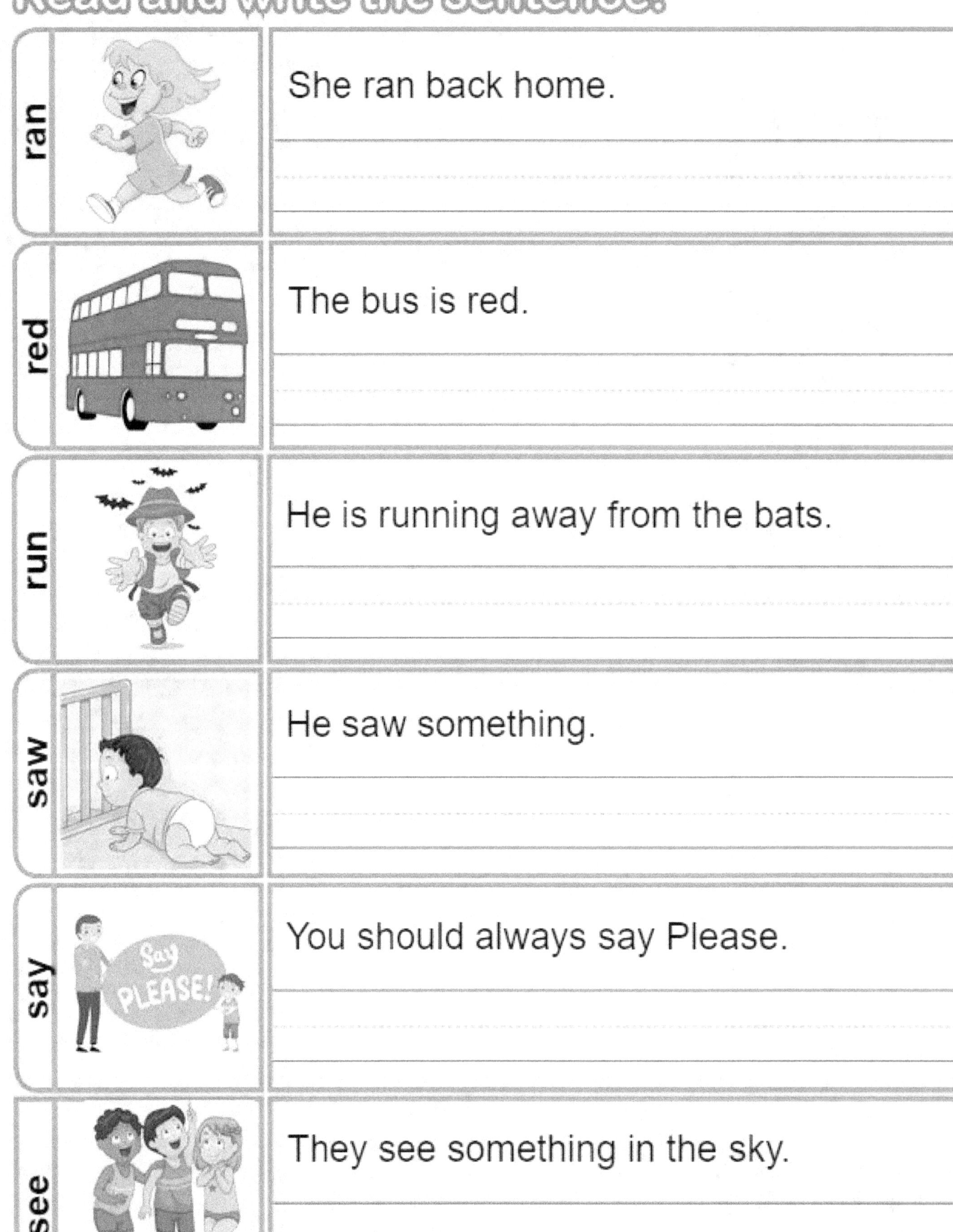

ran		She ran back home.
red		The bus is red.
run		He is running away from the bats.
saw		He saw something.
say		You should always say Please.
see		They see something in the sky.

Read
Trace
Write
she
elle
sit
asseoir
six
six
sun
soleil
ten
dix
the
une

Read and write the sentence!

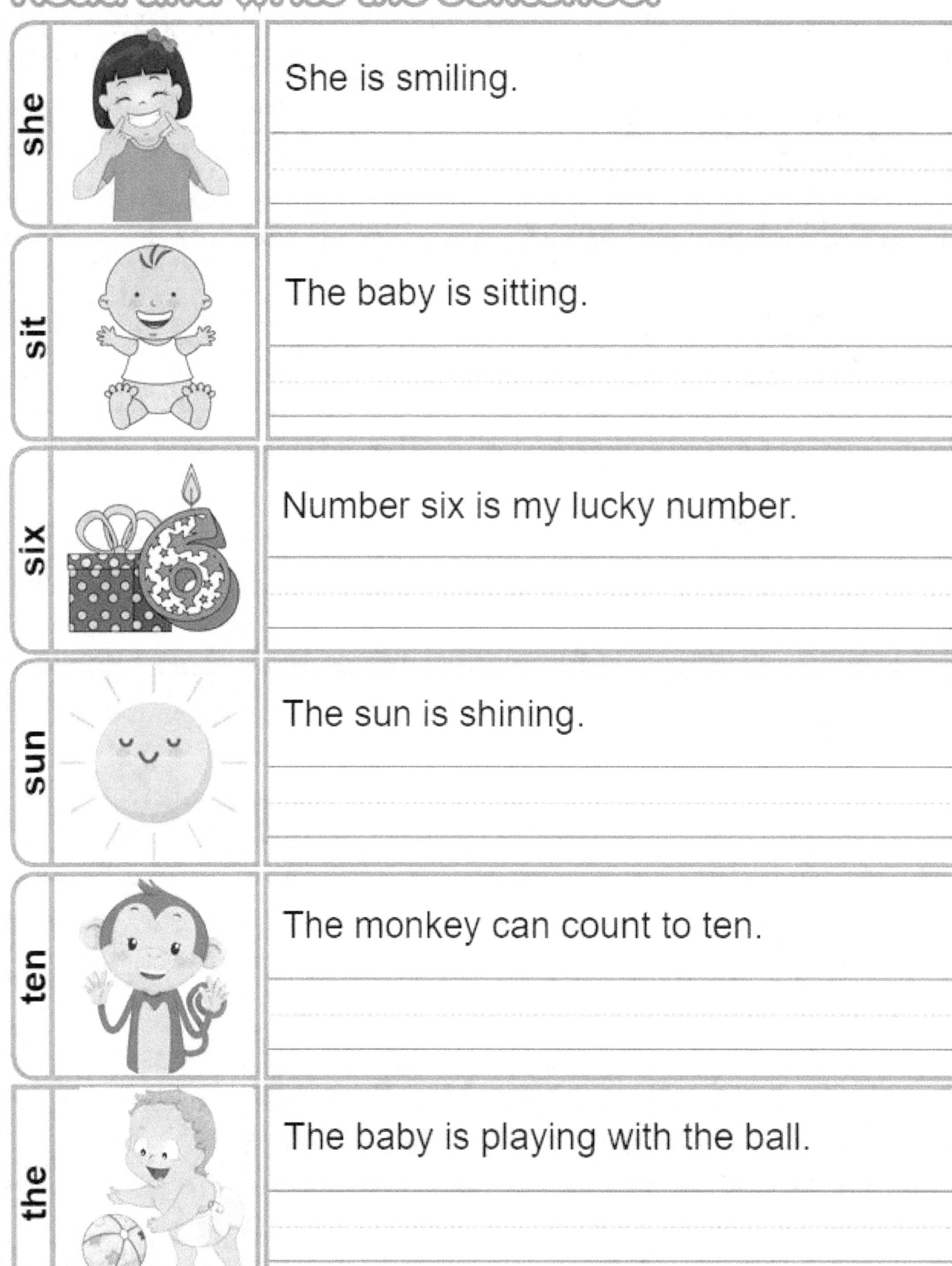

Read   Trace   Write

Read and write the sentence!

Read	Trace	Write
was était		
way façon		
who quoi		
why pourquoi		
yes oui		
you vous		

Read and write the sentence!

was	He was reading a book.
way	Let's go this way
who	Who wants to dance?
why	Why is the machine not working?
yes	Yes, I am so happy!
you	I love you!

Read
Trace
Write

away
un moyen

baby
bébé

back
retour

ball
balle

bear
ours

been
était

Read and write the sentence!

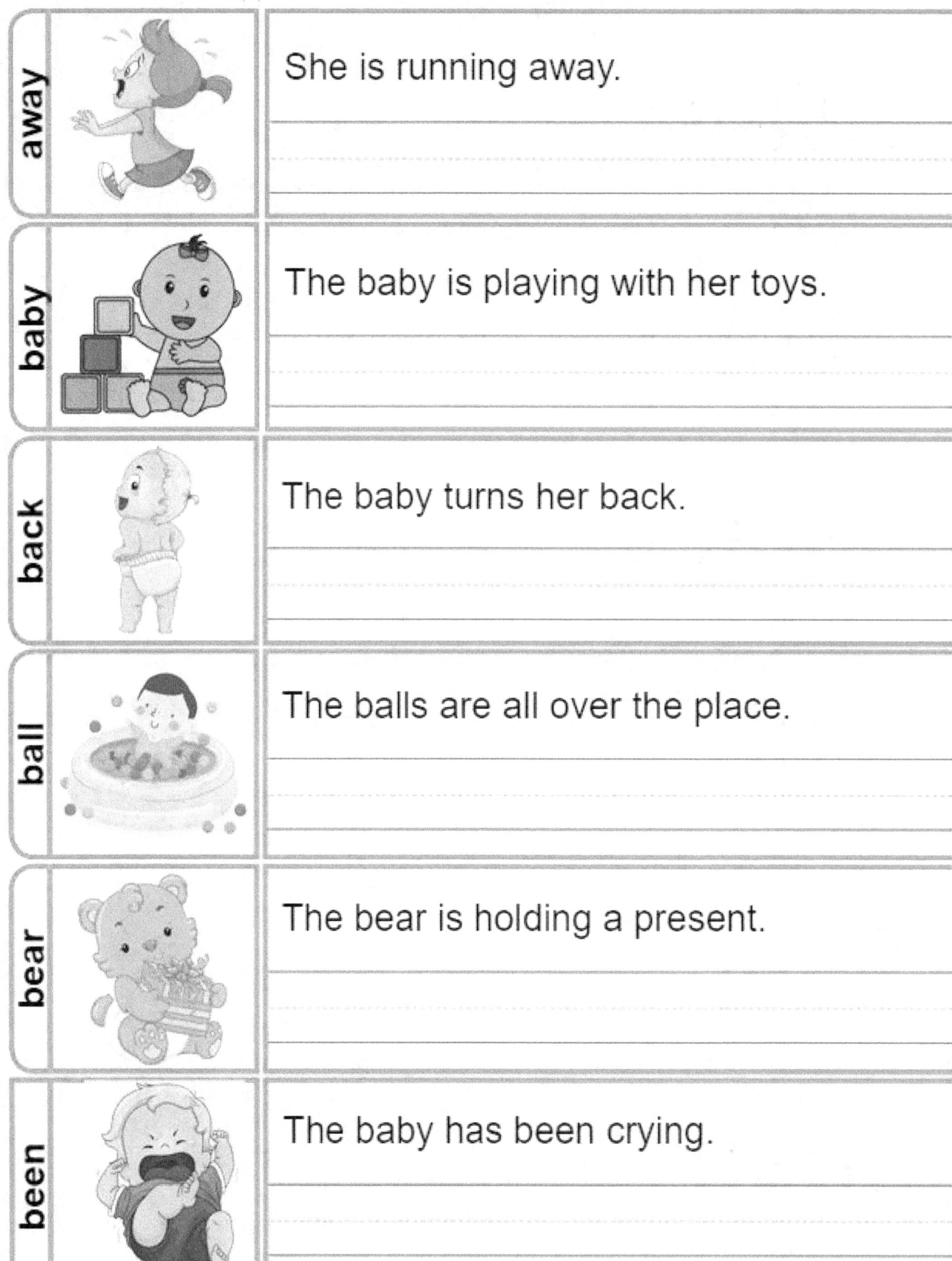

Read	Trace	Write
bell cloche		
best meilleur		
bird oiseau		
blue bleu		
boat bateau		
both tous les deux		

Read and write the sentence!

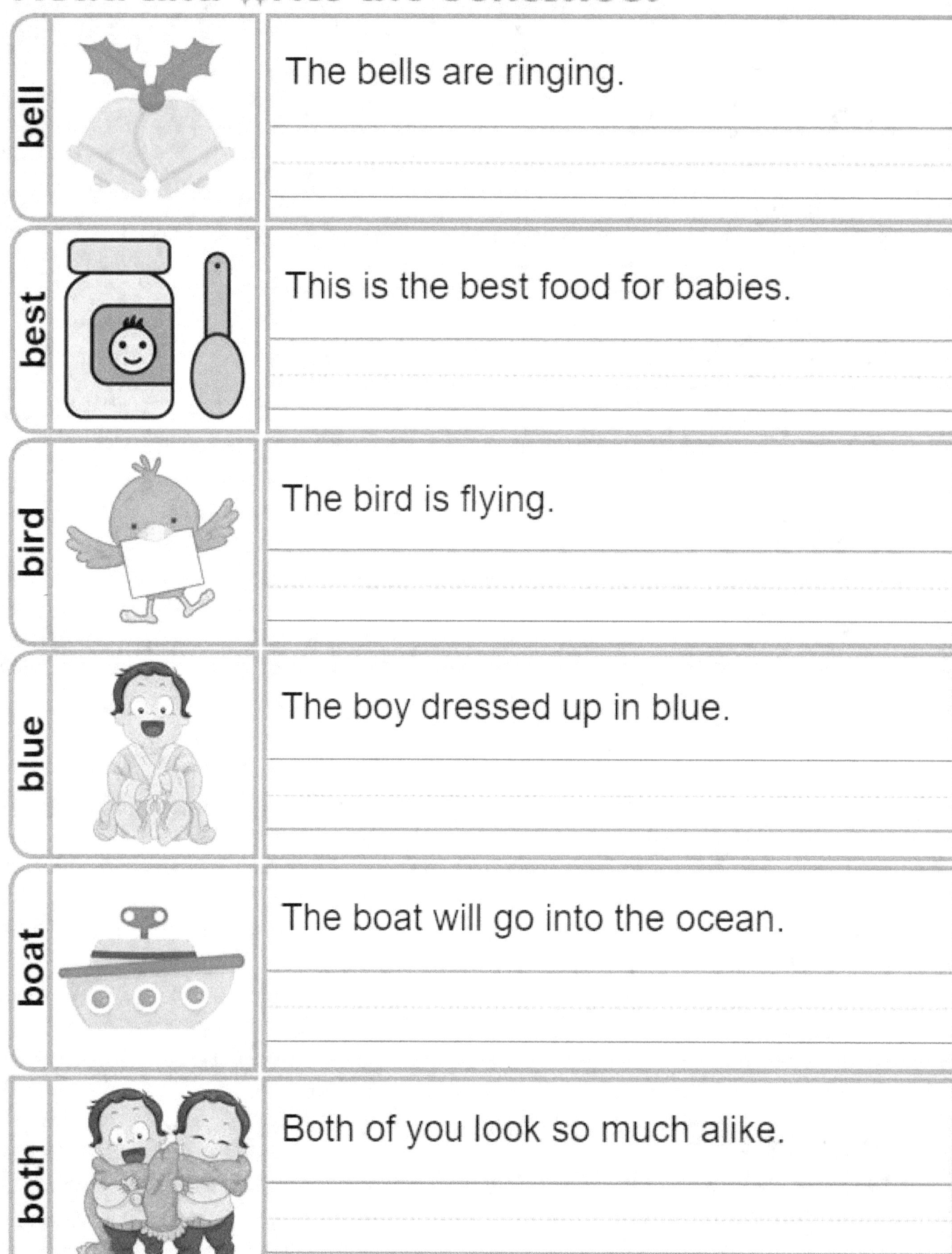

bell		The bells are ringing.
best		This is the best food for babies.
bird		The bird is flying.
blue		The boy dressed up in blue.
boat		The boat will go into the ocean.
both		Both of you look so much alike.

Read	Trace	Write
cake gâteau		
call appel		
came venu		
coat manteau		
cold du froid		
come viens		

Read and write the sentence!

cake	The cake is for your birthday.
call	She is calling for somebody.
came	She came with her bag.
coat	The girl is wearing her coat.
cold	The baby feels cold.
come	Come here to the slide!

Read	Trace	Write
corn blé		
does est-ce que		
doll poupée		
done terminé		
door porte		
down vers le bas		

Read and write the sentence!

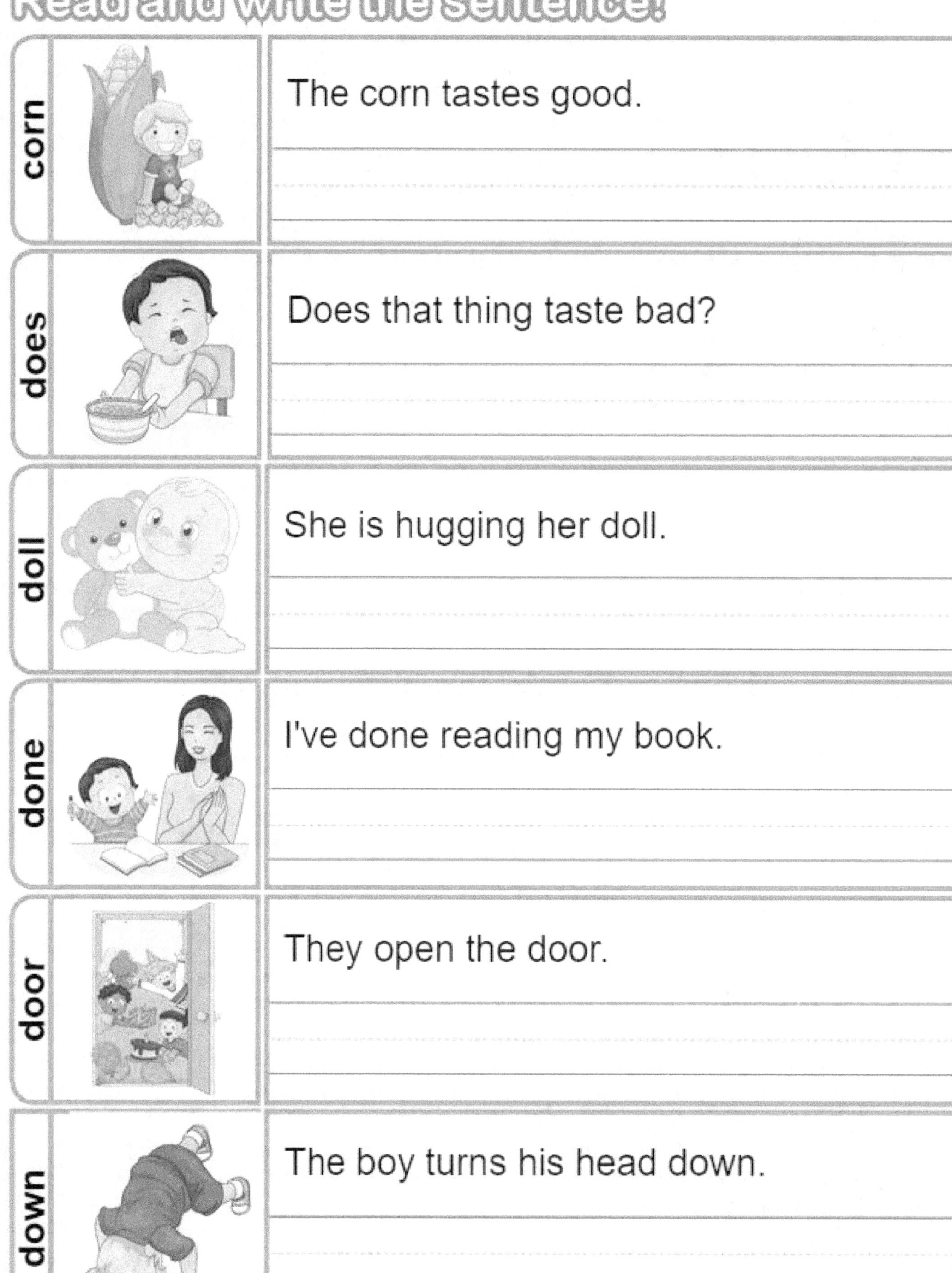

Read
Trace
Write
draw
dessiner
duck
canard
fall
tomber
farm
ferme
fast
vite
feet
pied

Read and write the sentence!

draw	They all draw pictures.
duck	The duck is yellow.
fall	He fell down from the swing.
farm	He grows crops at his farm.
fast	She is doing everything very fast.
feet	I touch my feet.

Read	Trace	Write
find trouver		
fire feu		
fish poisson		
five cinq		
four quatre		
from de		

Read and write the sentence!

find		They are finding something.
fire		The fire is blazing and dangerous.
fish		The fish are swimming in the ocean.
five		You get birthday gifts for turning five.
four		The lion is turning four today.
from		She will draw a picture of her flower.

Read	Trace	Write
full plein		
game jeu		
gave a donné		
girl fille		
give donner		
goes va		

Read and write the sentence!

full	His backpack is full of things.
game	This game is enjoyable.
gave	She gave something to her friend.
girl	The girl is sad because of something.
give	The baby gives her mommy something.
goes	She goes to the forest.

Read	Trace	Write
good bien		
grow croître		
hand main		
have avoir		
head tête		
help aidez-moi		

Read and write the sentence!

good	The baby is acting very well today.
grow	My plant will grow!
hand	My hand is touching the wall.
have	She will have lots of friends.
head	My head is round.
help	They help each other wash the clothes.

Read
Trace
Write
here
ici
hill
colline
hold
tenir
home
maison
hurt
blesser
into
dans

Read and write the sentence!

here	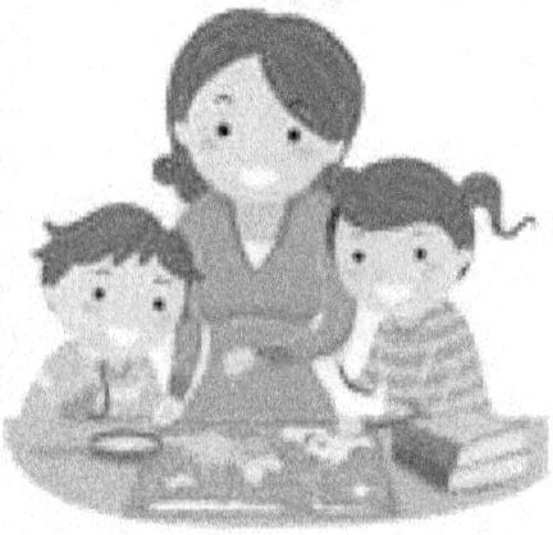	America is over here.
hill	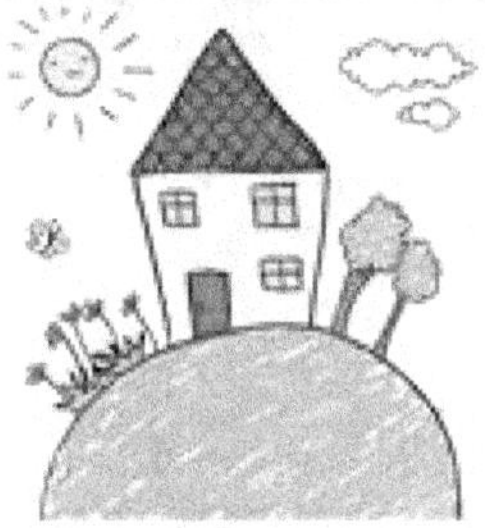	The hill has some trees and a house.
hold	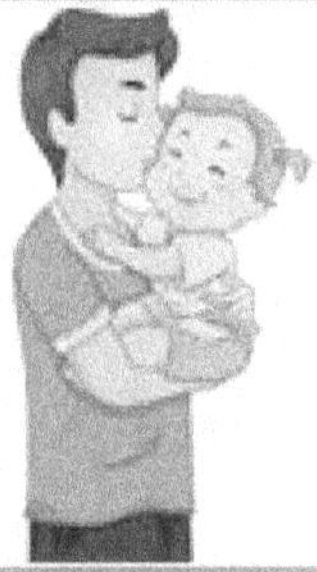	He is holding his daughter.
home	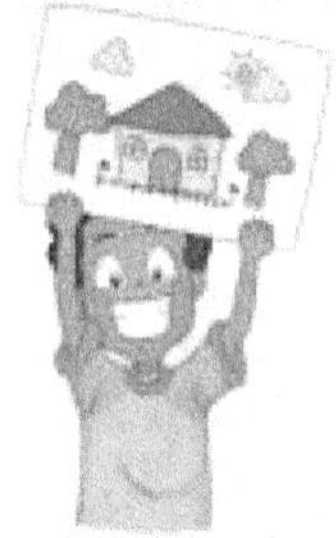	He drew a picture of his home.
hurt	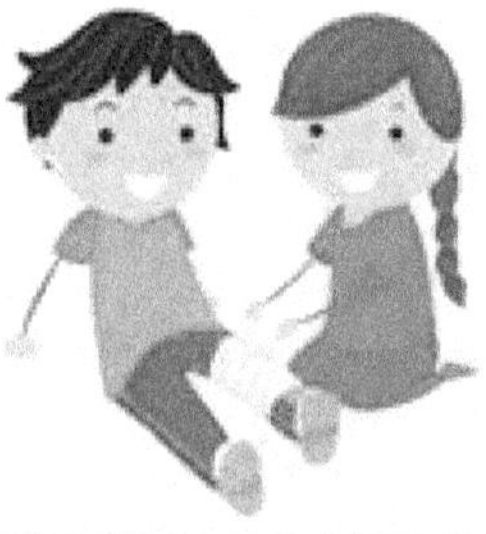	The boy is hurt.
into	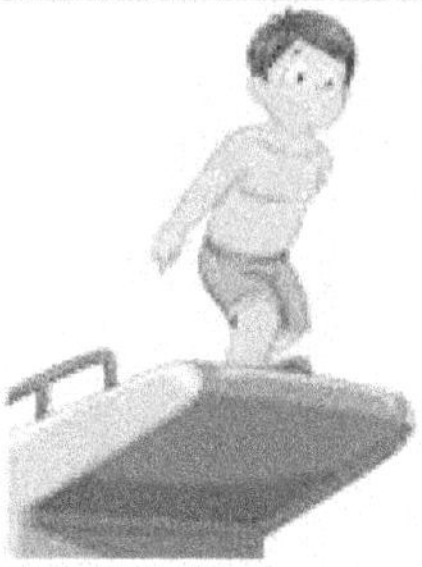	He will jump into the pool.

Read	Trace	Write
jump saut		
just juste		
keep garder		
kind gentil		
know savoir		
like comme		

jump — The cat jumped on the cushion.

just — The arrival of the plane just arrived.

keep — She keeps thinking about it.

kind — The woman is kind to the girl.

know — They know that they will go over there.

like — He likes to ride on the horse.

Read
Trace
Write
live
vivre
long
longue
look
regardez
made
fabriqué
make
fabriqué
many
beaucoup

Read and write the sentence!

live		They all live together.
long		The pencil is very long.
look		They are looking at something.
made		They made a promise.
make		They are going to make something.
many		He has many shirts.

Read	Trace	Write
milk lait		
much beaucoup		
must devoir		
name nom		
nest nid		
once une fois que		

Read and write the sentence!

milk		I have milk for breakfast.
much		I like to eat this very much.
must		I must do all my homework.
name		My name is Joe.
nest		The bird has a nest.
once		He once liked to look at his computer.

Read	Trace	Write
only seulement		
open ouvert		
over plus de		
pick choisir		
play jouer		
pull tirer		

only	There is only one student.
open	He wants to open the door.
over	The class is over.
pick	She picked up something.
play	They like to play together.
pull	She is pulling on her friend's hair.

Read	Trace	Write
rain pluie		
read lis		
ride balade		
ring bague		
said m'a dit		
seed la graine		

Read and write the sentence!

rain		The rain is not going to hit us.
read		She likes to read books.
ride		The baby is riding on a toy horse.
ring		The bird is holding a ring in its beak.
said		She said hello to her neighbor.
seed		The seeds are going to plant.

Read	Trace	Write
shoe chaussure		
show spectacle		
sing chanter		
snow neige		
some certains		
song chanson		

Read and write the sentence!

shoe	Her shoes are cute and purple.
show	This map shows the location.
sing	The baby can sing along.
snow	I like to play snow.
some	These are some of my toys.
song	I will sing a song in the talent show.

Read
Trace
Write
soon
bientôt
stop
arrêtez
take
prendre
tell
dire
that
cette
them
leur

Read and write the sentence!

soon		The eggs will hatch soon.
stop		The teacher says to stop.
take		They take some flowers.
tell		She is telling a story.
that		That bird dressed up as Santa.
them		He likes to eat them.

Read
Trace
Write
then
puis
they
ils
this
cette
time
temps
tree
arbre
upon
sur

Read and write the sentence!

then	Then, I will go to bed.
they	They are running to school.
this	This is my duck.
time	The time always moves on.
tree	There are lots of green trees in the park.
upon	Once upon a time, there was a princess.

Read	Trace	Write
very très		
walk marcher		
want vouloir		
warm chaud		
wash lavage		
well bien		

very		The baby is lovely.
walk		They are walking on the sidewalk.
want		The baby wants more milk.
warm		The bath is warm.
wash		She is going to wash the dishes.
well		He can save money well.

Read	Trace	Write
went est allé		
were sont		
what quoi		
when quand		
will volonté		
wind vent		

Read and write the sentence!

went		The crocodile went to the pond.
were		There were lots of toys.
what		What is the lion doing?
when		When are you going to wake up?
will		Will I get it in?
wind		The wind is blowing fiercely.

Read	Trace	Write
wish souhait		
with avec		
wood bois		
work travail		
your votre		
about à propos		

Read and write the sentence!

wish		I wish you a happy Christmas!
with		He is with his sister.
wood		He is stacking up wooden blocks.
work		He is going to work in his tractor.
your		Your baby is wearing a yellow suit.
about		It's about to be 12:30.

Read
Trace
Write
after
après
again
encore
apple
pomme
black
noir
bread
pain
bring
apporter

after		The teacher calmed them after they fought.
again		He did it again!
apple		The apple is red and juicy.
black		The crow is black.
bread		My breakfast is bread and jam.
bring		He is bringing his project.

Read	Trace	Write
brown marron		
carry porter		
chair chaise		
clean nettoyer		
could pourrait		
don't ne fais pas		

Read and write the sentence!

brown	Her stuffed animal is a brown bear.
carry	He is carrying a big crayon.
chair	He is sitting on his chair.
clean	He needs to clean up.
could	The baby could do push-ups.
don't	Don't do that!

Read	Trace	Write
drink boisson		
eight huit		
every chaque		
first première		
floor sol		
found a trouvé		

Read and write the sentence!

drink	The baby likes to drink water.
eight	You get eight gifts for turning eight!
every	Every book is colorful.
first	We won first place.
floor	She is sitting on the floor.
found	It found a hat in the streets.

Read
Trace
Write
funny
drôle
going
aller
grass
herbe
green
vert
horse
cheval
house
maison

Read and write the sentence!

funny	The rabbit thinks the joke is funny.
going	The bear is going to eat all the honey.
grass	The goat eats grass on the hill.
green	The turtle that is walking is green.
horse	The horse is magical.
house	They lived in that house.

Read	Trace	Write
kitty chat		
laugh rire		
light lumière		
money argent		
never jamais		
night nuit		

Read and write the sentence!

kitty	The kitties are charming.
laugh	They are laughing while playing.
light	The boy will turn on the lights.
money	I have earned a lot of money.
never	The bear never ate ice cream before.
night	I will sleep on my blanket at night.

Read	Trace	Write
paper papier		
party fête		
right correct		
round rond		
seven sept		
shall doit		

Read and write the sentence!

paper	I will draw on the paper for a project.
party	The party will be for her birthday.
right	They say we have to go right.
round	The frogs' eyes are round.
seven	The monkey can count to seven.
shall	Shall I make a garden?

Read	Trace	Write
sheep mouton		
sleep dormir		
small petit		
start début		
stick des bâtons		
table table		

Read and write the sentence!

sheep		The sheep have a bell around its neck.
sleep		I will go to sleep in my comfortable bed.
small		The small baby will crawl to its crib.
start		She will start sleeping soon.
stick		He has some sticks to play.
table		The table has a toy on it.

Read
Trace
Write
thank
remercier
their
leur
there
là
these
celles-ci
thing
chose
think
pense

Read and write the sentence!

thank		He made a Thank you card for you.
their		They will enjoy their picnic.
there		There is something in front of you.
these		These are my eating material.
thing		The thing is broken.
think		She thinks about what she is going to draw.

Read
Trace
Write
those
ceux
three
trois
today
aujourd'hui
under
en dessous de
watch
regarder
water
l'eau

those		Those are mine.
three		She will turn three today.
today		Today is a beautiful day.
under		The puppy sleeps under the blanket.
watch		They both watch the video.
water		He is drinking water after a long soccer game.

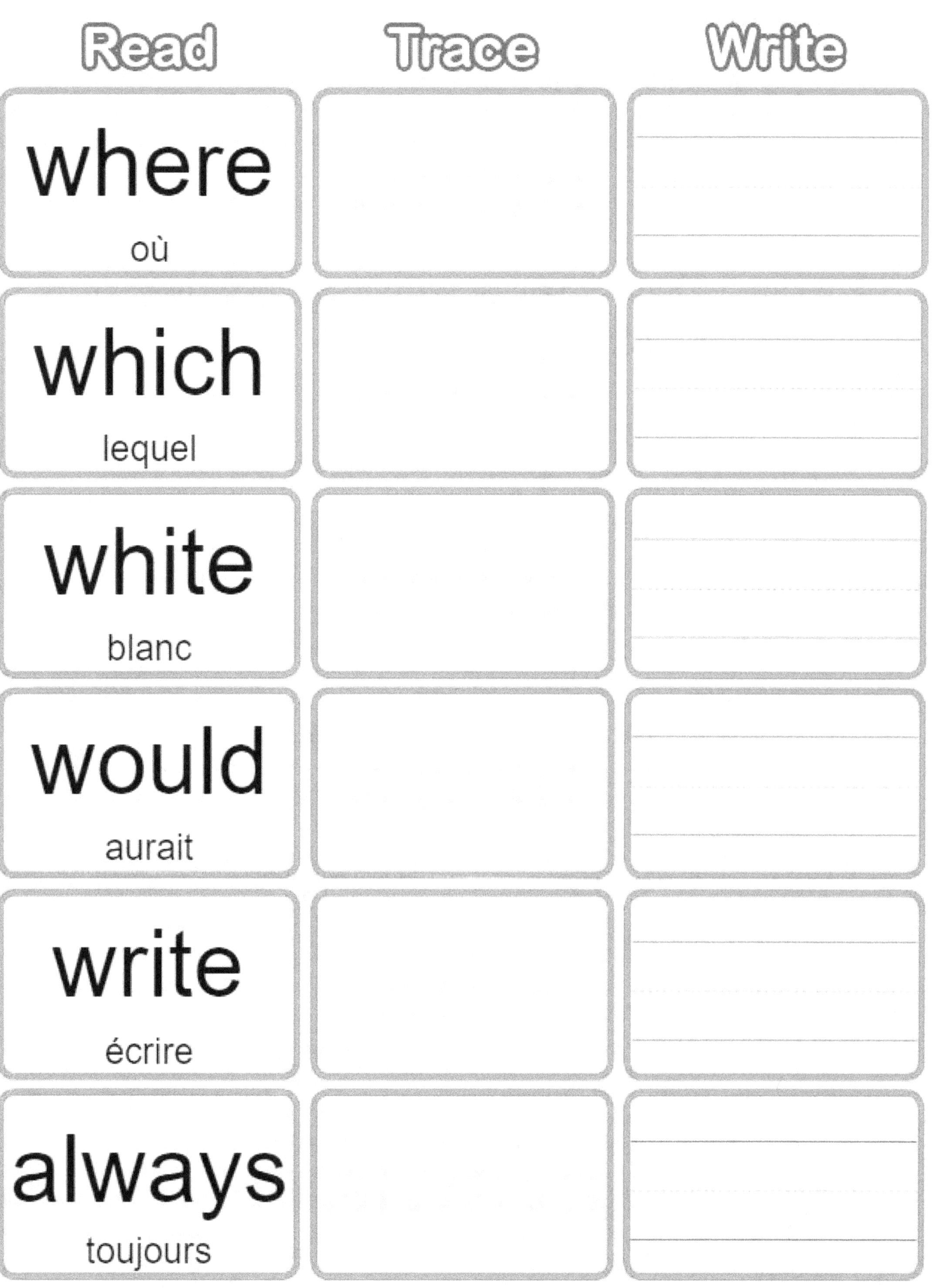

Read
Trace
Write
where
où
which
lequel
white
blanc
would
aurait
write
écrire
always
toujours

Read and write the sentence!

where	Where are we?
which	The clothes which are my sisters are colorful.
white	The sheep have white wool.
would	He would tell them a story.
write	I like to write lots of stories.
always	I am always happy that it is Christmas.

Read	Trace	Write
around environ		
before avant		
better meilleur		
farmer fermier		
father père		
flower fleur		

Read and write the sentence!

around	I will shuffle the shapes around.
before	Before I go to school, I kiss my mom.
better	I can make it better.
farmer	The farmer takes care of the animals.
father	My father is wearing a blue shirt.
flower	She will play with the flowers.

Read	Trace	Write
garden jardin		
ground sol		
letter des lettres		
little peu		
mother mère		
myself moi même		

garden	Her garden is vast and healthy.
ground	I am playing with my dog on the ground.
letter	These are the letters A, B, and C.
little	The world is small.
mother	My mother is very nice.
myself	I made these by myself.

Read	Trace	Write
please s'il vous plaît		
pretty joli		
rabbit lapin		
school école		
sister sœur		
street rue		

Read and write the sentence!

please	Please stop pulling my hair.
pretty	She made the cake very pretty.
rabbit	The rabbit is white and soft.
school	This is the school.
sister	My sister is wearing a pink dress.
street	They are walking across the street.

Read	Trace	Write
window fenêtre		
yellow jaune		
because parce que		
brother frère		
chicken poulet		
goodbye au revoir		

Read and write the sentence!

window — The window is open.

yellow — The ducky is yellow.

because — She will sleep because it is night.

brother — His brother is playing with him.

chicken — The chicken has hatched out of the egg.

goodbye — The animal is saying goodbye.

Read	Trace	Write
morning matin		
picture image		
birthday anniversaire		
children les enfants		
squirrel écureuil		
together ensemble		

Read and write the sentence!

morning	He likes to ride his bike in the morning.
picture	He will take a picture.
birthday	Today is my birthday!
children	The children are doing something.
squirrel	The squirrel is cute.
together	They are sharing a bed together.